My Cow

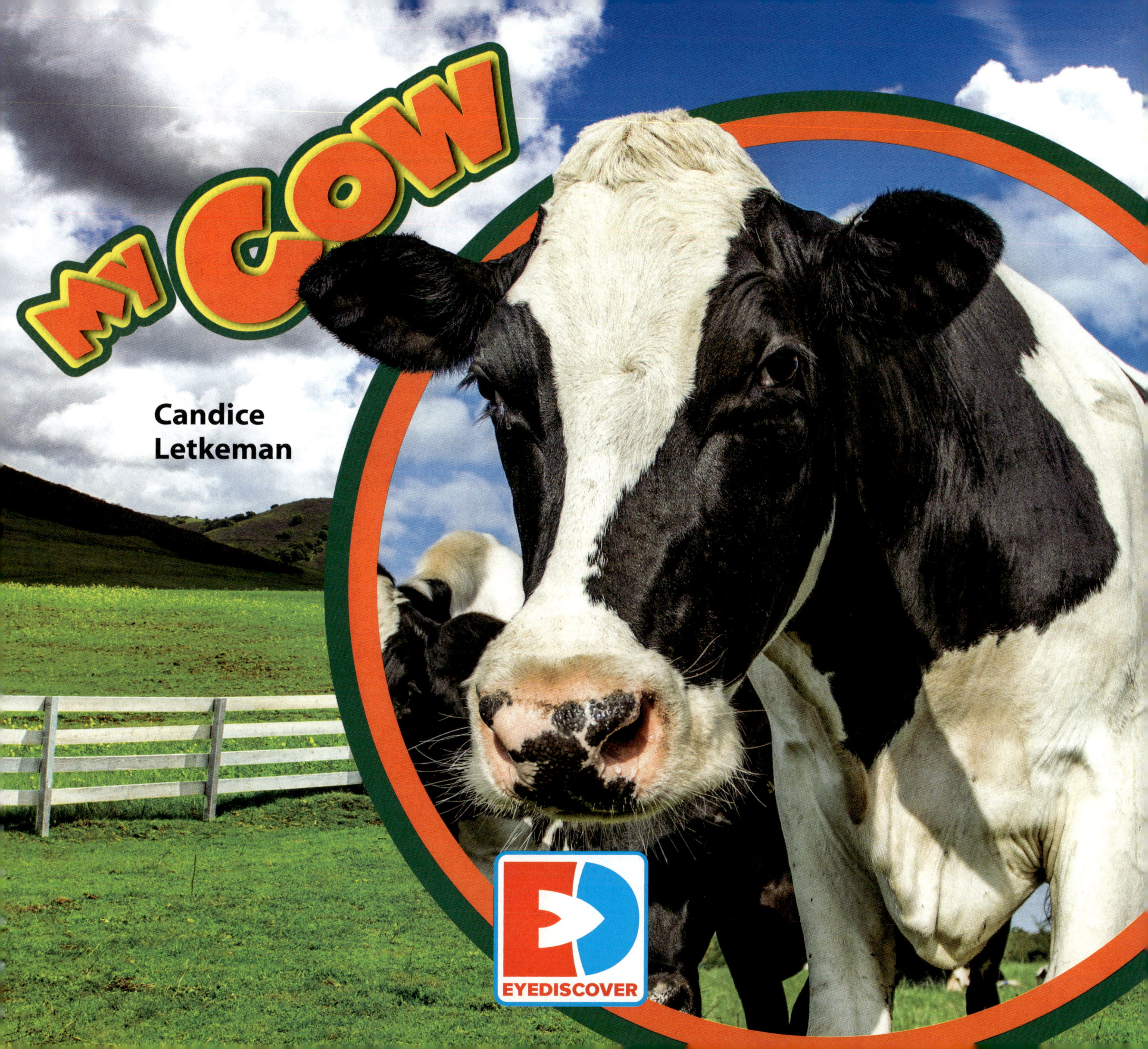

Candice
Letkeman

Go to www.eyediscover.com and enter this book's unique code.

BOOK CODE

L363443

EYEDISCOVER brings you optic readalongs that support active learning.

Published by AV² by Weigl
350 5th Avenue, 59th Floor New York, NY 10118
Website: www.eyediscover.com

Library of Congress Control Number: 2017930606

ISBN 978-1-4896-5650-6 (hardcover)

Printed in the United States of America
in Brainerd, Minnesota
1 2 3 4 5 6 7 8 9 0 21 20 19 18 17

072017
020317

Editor: Katie Gillespie
Designer: Mandy Christiansen

Weigl acknowledges Getty Images, Alamy, iStock, and Shutterstock as the primary image suppliers for this title.

EYEDISCOVER provides enriched content, optimized for tablet use, that supplements and complements this book. EYEDISCOVER books strive to create inspired learning and engage young minds in a total learning experience.

Watch
Video content brings each page to life.

Browse
Thumbnails make navigation simple.

Read
Follow along with text on the screen.

Listen
Hear each page read aloud.

Your EYEDISCOVER Optic Readalongs come alive with...

Audio
Listen to the entire book read aloud.

Video
High resolution videos turn each spread into an optic readalong.

OPTIMIZED FOR
- ✓ TABLETS
- ✓ WHITEBOARDS
- ✓ COMPUTERS
- ✓ AND MUCH MORE!

MY COW
In this book, you will learn about
• how they look
• what they do
• what they eat
and much more!

Cows help feed the world. Milk comes from cows. Ice cream, cheese, and yogurt are made from milk.

6

Cows need to be milked twice a day. It takes 350 squirts from a cow's udder to get 1 gallon of milk.

Cows eat grass all day. A cow's stomach has four compartments.

Cows are very social animals. They moo to each other. Cows form close bonds with a few members of the herd.

Cows make enough saliva to fill a big trash can each day. Cows lick their calves even after they are grown.

A cow can run faster than a horse in deep mud.

Some cows have short horns. Other cows have long horns. A cow's horns can be longer than a bed.

Cows do not have top front teeth. They curl their tongues around grass and pull it because they can not bite it.

Cows are in the same family as bison, antelopes, sheep, and goats.

A cow **sits down** and **stands up** **14 times a day**.

There are **more than 1 billion cows** in the world today.

No two cows' spots are exactly the **same**.

A **cow** drinks
up to 50 gallons
of water each day.
That is almost enough
to fill a **bathtub.** (189 liters)

Cows can **smell** things up
to **5 miles away**.
(8 kilometers)

Cows usually have
one calf
at a time.
Sometimes, they have **twins**.

KEY WORDS

Research has shown that as much as 65 percent of all written material published in English is made up of 300 words. These 300 words cannot be taught using pictures or learned by sounding them out. They must be recognized by sight. This book contains 50 common sight words to help young readers improve their reading fluency and comprehension. This book also teaches young readers several important content words, such as proper nouns. These words are paired with pictures to aid in learning and improve understanding.

Page	Sight Words First Appearance
5	and, are, comes, from, help, made, the, world
7	a, be, day, get, it, need, of, takes, to
8	all, eat, four, has
10	animals, close, each, few, other, they, very, with
12	after, big, enough, even, grown, make, their
15	can, in, run, than
16	have, long, some
19	around, because, do, not
20	as, family, same

Page	Content Words First Appearance
5	cheese, cows, ice cream, milk, yogurt
7	gallon, squirts, udder
8	compartments, grass, stomach
10	bonds, herd, members
12	calves, saliva, trash can
15	horse, mud
16	bed, horns
19	grass, teeth, tongues
20	antelopes, bison, goats, sheep

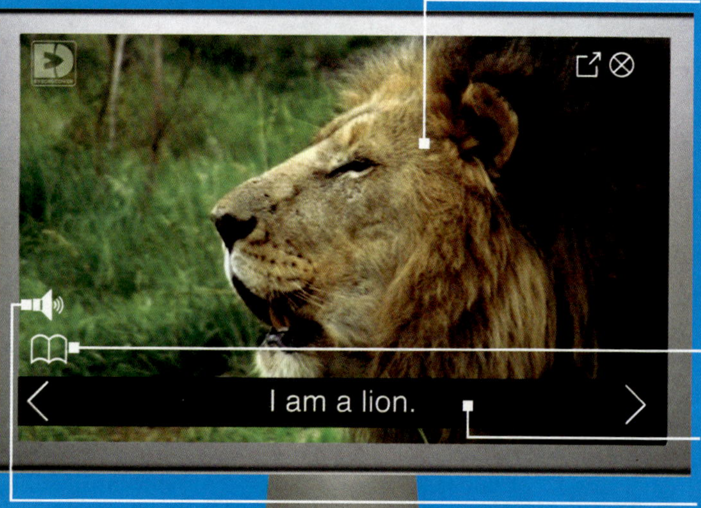

Watch
Video content brings each page to life.

Browse
Thumbnails make navigation simple.

Read
Follow along with text on the screen.

Listen
Hear each page read aloud.

Go to www.eyediscover.com and enter this book's unique code.

BOOK CODE

L363443